Death of Hardship

Ekpe Inyang

Langaa Research & Publishing CIG
Mankon, Bamenda

Publisher
Langaa RPCIG
Langaa Research & Publishing Common Initiative Group
P.O. Box 902 Mankon
Bamenda
North West Region
Cameroon
Langaagrp@gmail.com
www.langaa-rpcig.net

Distributed in and outside N. America by African Books Collective
orders@africanbookscollective.com
www.africanbookcollective.com

ISBN: 9956-727-51-2

DISCLAIMER
All views expressed in this publication are those of the author and do not necessarily reflect the views of Langaa RPCIG.

Table of Contents

iv

Foreword

Ekpe Inyang's *Death of Hardship* is a sixty-one poem collection which exemplifies man's relationship with the natural environment. The poems articulate the fact that our immediate environment is an invaluable source of wealth for humanity. From "Desert's Lesson" to "Beyond Human Destruction," the poet successfully articulates the point that we can utilize our environment to put an end to all hardship. He does, indeed, re-echo Jonathan Edward's "The Way to Wealth," but goes further to lambast and condemn all dictatorial regimes which mismanage human and environmental resources thereby leaving the masses to persistently wallow in misery and hardship. When he cautions us to 'Drag you your steps to borrow/Reduce your mounts of sorrow,' he appears to sound a warning note to dictators in "Beware Tyranny" because they blindfold their subjects by turning "black into white" and preventing them from enjoying the immensurable wealth that 'lies within [the] cosmos' (p.76).

Inyang's poetry puts him across as a family man, a seasoned traveler, a devoted environmentalist, and a keen observer of life. His admiration for his lovely daughter, Offy, comes across in "Mother Offy" and "Hope's Long Journey." In "The Flight" and poems about the Diaspora such as "Incommunicado" and "The Return," we come to recognize the fact that the poet's numerous trips abroad have helped him learn a lot in spite of the nostalgic feelings when he is away from home. One gets the feeling that his wealth of knowledge in environmental NGOs has not only shaped him into an ardent lover of nature but has also made him produce poetry which is unique in form and content. Just like the environmental diversity of nature is diverse, so too is his poetry varied: free verse, blank verse, metrical poetry, and calligrammes. The manner in which Inyang venerates Nature and the Environment in poems such as "Storm," "The Moon," and "Beyond Human Destruction" qualifies him to be styled an apostle of "New Romanticism."

All in all, *Death of Hardship* is diversified in the titles of its poems, but unified in the oneness of its voice, its persona, and its themes. There is a single voice in the poems that speaks to children, men, and women from all strata of society on a variety of themes which, inexorably, culminate into one call—the call of all of us to manage our Environment sustainably in order to declare an end to hardships. *Death of Hardship* is a must-read collection for all and sundry. By the way, it comes as no surprise that Inyang in "Read A Poem," prescribes poetry as a panacea to all of humanity's problems. Hear him:

> Read a poem at noontime, and
> You guarantee your moral sanity;
> This is self-expurgating bleach,
> An aid for you to play well your great societal role
> (p.46)

Ba'bila Mutia, April 20
Dramatist, poet, and lecturer of Literature and Creative Writi
Ecole Normale Supérieur (ENS), Yaoun

vi

Desert's Lesson

26 March 2011

Kill not your dream for property
In dire climes of poverty

Visions there are of mounts of foods
When times are plagued with heavy floods

Desert is great lesson to learn
Strategies there are always to earn

Depend you less on humans
Bare rocks may find no humus

Count more on your own toil
Never your hands ever to soil

Drag you your steps to borrow
Reduce your mounts of sorrow

Opt you for schemes that yield
Always your fame to build

Completely Red

26 March 2011

Time it was to go
Much before Sun peeped
Another feather to add
Plumage kept across the seas

Clear dew in his heavy lids
A lump heavy in his cage
Lead was his hand to wave
Leaving behind his ten-month lass

Deep in his heart
The thought of it was hard
Tough to believe
It wasn't a false step

Fireside was clearly cold
Energy source was drowned
Reward for venturing
A weightier plume to add

A bold step he took
Filled with agony and joy
A year of bruising pain
A gain for more years than one

Sweated he did indeed
His household to maintain
Toiling for feather in yonder land
Eking out on generosity of aid

Came that gray day
His balance sheet completely red

Vibration from his belt, and he picked
His better-half it was

The moon's too young
My honey to expect
It's well below water table
Our pail's completely dry

How then will I to home
My folder now thus empty
Honey, I'm tongue-tight struck
This moment see I red

No panic, my sweetie pie
Straight you to where you roost
It's such a hard dream though
The harsh drought to address

Went he straight to the podium
Where at Sunrise he mounted
Hitting the rock for moisture
My gosh! Green light he got!

Incommunicado

26 March 2011

Moons had passed, no news
But from those that no news brought
My baby left still babbling
First time out with care left behind

The burden too heavy to bear
Sought I a way for home to reach
No radio means, no mobile means
Not even Internet

No word across the ocean
To thaw the ice in me
Worried about my homestead
Knowing the well I left was fast drying up

The Return

10 April 2011

Like leaving Sodom
And heading straight for
Gomorrah!

A huge red feather
Plucked across the ocean
Clearly displayed on his head;

Great threat to Leopard,
A few feeble whiskers on the head;
No match for the red feather.

No space for him to near
Leopard Trembles his sight to stand;
The stool now was clearly for him.

Fate of Cockroaches

9 April 2011

Multitudinous crevices,
Labyrinth of utter darkness,
Paradise for Cockroaches,
Opportunistic creatures exuding hateful fumes,
Nocturnal vectors of leprous products,
Toxins for sane minds,
Dishes for ravenous Crocodiles.

Clipped-winged Eagle, from yonder land, lost in transit,
Got stuck, on sudden descent, in maze of coarse crevices
Decorating den of Lilliputian-Leopard,
Head-Crocodile, Master of Acclaimed Cockroaches.

Left with fewer choices than one,
Eagle-On-Descent the soot-dressed crevices embraced,
Its form and size concealed to survive,
Its volume reduced, flattened the space to fit, and crawled:
Nebuchadnezzar-show-of-abeyance to Lilliput-Leopard,
Despotic rogue, con-Coach of caged-Cockroaches.

Piece of hard Purok-wood
Buried in Odnowe-pool of crook-Crocodiles
Lies there centuries long,
Turning not into Crocodile;
Eagle now in crevice-maze seemingly glued,
Its wits and prowess deployed in haste, found its wings,
Soared high, skill-bombarding den, crushing acclaimed Cockroaches,
Now in mid-air, dangling at noontime, their utter flatness exposed,
Bleeding blood of shame, spelling dire doom even for HC-MAC.

ESD Cameroon

(Composed with the generous contribution of words by ESD Cameroon workshop participants, the poets behind the poet)

18 April 2011

Education for what?
Sustainable Development.
ESD approach so rare,
So distant yet so near.

Gunilla went on Marathon
ESD seeds to bring;
Today we are in Yaounde,
ESD seeds to sow.

Before the dream was hazy
Today so real the seeds,
Timely and reassuring,
Inspiring us to action.

A pyramid to build:
Ecology, society,
Economy, that's it,
With solid rocks from Sweden.

Swedish team simply fabulous:
Gunilla, Per, Staffan,
And Zipporah from Kenya,
A team so down-to-earth.

Team resourceful and practical,
Discussions participative,
With Ministers and Delegates
And Teachers of Our Children.

World Wide Fund for Nature
Great Programme - CCPO
Set the great ball in motion
ESD seeds to sow.

Such free and fair debate!
Exciting, informative,
Revealing and terrific:
ESD Team, O yeah!

The task was so challenging,
Discussions so enriching,
Exciting, fun and thrilling,
Educative, so relevant.

Great Head of the Environment
And Nature Protection, and of Forestry
And Wildlife, propped up by those of Basic,
And Secondary Education.

ESD seeds they blessed,
18/4/2011.
Positive, reassuring,
ESD seeds are sown!

Oh, no! Two questions have I for you:
Who will the nursery water?
Who will the seedlings tend
Cam-schools to green to turn?

Seven Hills Away

10 May 2011

Hammers, mallets,
Chisels on his head;
Incessant banging,
Head palpitating
Like heart of frightened toad;
Chest wheezing,
Breathing hard and tight;
Body trembling,
Shivering like leaf;
Head like fire,
Palms and soles
More like ice;
Nose and eyes
Running like stream;
Force behind
Hard to know;
Clear the need for Doctor;
Doctor's house
Thousands of miles,
Medicine store
Seven hills away.

Where White Is Black

24 May 2011

Where white is black
And black is white
What else can you expect?
Right is left,
And left right;
Front is back,
And back front;
In is out,
And out in;
Up is down,
And down up;
Tall is short,
And short tall;
Big is small,
And small big;
Strong is weak,
And weak strong;
Sharp is blunt,
And blunt sharp;
Such is the kind of
World we often meet.

Double Shadows

24 May 2011

Chats in whispers,
Sound of pacing feet,
Feeble minds buried
Behind bolted doors.

Double shadows
Clear on the floor,
One ash colour, one purely dark,
Cast by luminous sky-ball.

Light so bright,
Beautiful from the sky
Which is but sea of soot
Before twisted eyes.

Double anthems song
Under a flag flying high,
Displaying double shadows,
Thin elongations on the floor.

Come see the shadows,
But tell not the story;
Dance along with it,
Hold it close to your chest.

Fakoship

28 May 2011

Fakoship even in heavy rains!
Of hard wood she's surely made;
Red wood, black wood,
Not white wood,
Though in white dressed.

Limbe-Calabar Atlantic stretch
Sails she steady on course,
Despite the turbulent tossing
And frequent, frightful banging,
Falls from wavy mounts.

Lifted suddenly high in air,
Dropped down abruptly again;
Ripples torturously wild,
Heart-breaking sight and sound,
Clear monsters warring at sea.

Stirring, rolling really wild,
Ahead mountains so tall,
Left and right valleys scary deep;
Like monsters ready to devour
Even the wildest beast.

But on sails Fakoship,
Faster than Leopard in hunt-chase,
Wilder than the sea monsters,
Crushing their rolling, confronting heads,
Ignoring their gory armpits left and right.

Wicked Call

05 June 2011

Each now picked up a tiny cell
Something I couldn't really tell
HE walked towards the gate of hell
Response to sound of wicked bell
Finger on trigger poised to shell
We hear the sounds as they now swell
Rivers and seas a bloody dell
What a grave image we now sell
All because of a tiny well

Sick Memories

9 June 2011

Go home I must
Cried he so hard,
After those lonesome days
Across Ocean of Ivory Tower
A red feather to procure
In hard currency

But then back home
Met he in shock
Climatic change
A prize to pay
In harder currency

Memories of it he wishes
Completely his mind can raze
As bread was rock
And water dust
Comfort a clear miscreant

A restart button to find
Much like fetching the moon
Reflected in the deep, deep sea
Temptations soaring for dire means
A start-up disk to find

His pride completely gone
Replaced by pauper's palm
Survival instincts so strong
Searching for start-up disk

Sweet Sound

10 June 2011

Early morning
My lids still heavy
Soft drums on rooftop
Like sweet guitar sound
Dandling and lulling me abed
To stare impending famine in the face
Nor thought nor hurrying move for early rise

Hope's Long Journey

11 June 2011

It was truly rocky,
Battle really long,
Hope nearly lost,
Supplications a flood;

Canoe dangling wild,
Tossed by the waves,
Ferryman ready,
Paddle in hand;

Fare really high,
Me to ferry 'cross,
The ocean so wide
To mountaintop;

Dream will surely come,
Though taking so long
To put on the sail,

Hope nearly lost;

Seven years gone,
Came June 11, Pentecost,
Offy's face shown,
Mummy-in-new-dress;

Life's first cry she gave,
Clear message of hope,
Arrival of part-fare
To put on the sail;
Hope's long journey,
Though ferryman so prompt
You to ferry 'cross
To mountaintop.

The Moon

23 June 2011

A clear sound of music approaching
I peeped out and espied your splendid form
Of diamond your face is surely made
Glittering so bright, sending me giddy
Stand still let me behold those eyes
Such a symmetrical display of perfection
The mesmerising roundness of your face
Such visage speaking of untold beauty lifts me high
That broad smile each time I behold you
The steady glow of delight in those eyes
So distinct from a swelling cloud of doubt
The very hue of which amplifies your form
And I see lit candles studded all about you
Dissipating the cloud, paying abeyance to you
Creating a celestial aura around you
And I see you standing at a temple high
Offering a long sermon of reality and promise
Instilling joy and hope in my fading heart
Clear music in those steps: sounds of flutes and harps
Sounds of xylophones and drums
A blend of cacophony and melody
This time slow, next time fast
This time of low pitch, next of high
And I get this strong feeling
I must quicken my steps, as I've come of age
And I charted my way to the sacred grove
In rhythm with the ceaseless throb of drums

The Flight

24 June 2011

I
Eagle with wings spread out like Iroko branches
Standing tall while its belly is being stuffed
I see items of various shapes and sizes
Eagle ready for migration, so to speak
Then us in a line like soldier-ants
Climbing way up above the wings
Walking straight into its copious tummy

II
Eagle's belly's nothing but a conference hall
Ushered in I am to take my seat
"Enjoy your flight, Sir", a lady says to me
And soon Eagle roars and turns around
Then comes the first lesson of the day
"Here you have…There you find…
This is how to…, just in case….
And ensure you are fastened to your seat"

III
Now Eagle faces a great lane for a race
This time running faster than before
Then gradually slows down to listen
As if in wait for a command to Go!
And suddenly it plunges into the race
And off the ground it shoots right into space
Making my heart jump hard as it does
Its beak pointing skyward as it flies
Its legs folded against its chest in the flight

IV

Looking down beneath I see roofs
Melting gradually into the abyss
And soon Eagle tears across a hazy sea above
And I find myself completely lost in space
Then suddenly we are above the hazy sea
In space with hazy carpet of sundry hues below
Surely a conference hall for celestial beings
And there terrestrial beings venture to go

V

It is a spectacle to glide above the seas
A sea of green and then of blue
And finally an endless one of brown
With very few patches of green and blue
And gradually we're above the hazy sea again
And then comes the second lesson of the day
"Ensure you are fastened to your seat"
Then Eagle goes, beak pointing to the earth
A tumbling race across the hazy sea

VI

Suddenly I can see millions of roofs again
Eagle turns and points its beak towards the lane
Unfolds its legs, ready to touch the ground
And everyone is breathless as we sit
Obviously praying to alight in one piece
And finally it is right on the lane
But now running in uncontrollable speed
Gradually the speed's under control
And it starts to glide to a final stop

Coincidence
(for Ben Okri)

26 June 2011

Over twenty years
since
they met face-to- face.

They are (or were?)
such great friends.

Sundown.
And Femi is sitting
on his balcony
overlooking the sea,
to catch some breeze,
his wife beside him,
introspecting.

They've just dropped
this strange discussion about life,
its meaning,
its essence,
its reality;
how,

after their children out-grow the house,
they might be
all alone again,
left to themselves
a great part of their dying days.
With no real friends around,
no great relatives,
except leeches and vampires,
what would life really mean?

Femi stares awhile,
has this strange feeling,
a premonition,
a presence of
the most unexpected being.

"What?" asks his wife.

"Nothing"

Silence.

"Where could Daniel be now,
if he's still part
of the reality of life?"

"Someone comes, honey", says his wife.

"One of those intruders, I guess."
But, behold,...

...Solomon comes.

In unison, they rise:
"What a Coincidence!"
And Solomon explains:
"Coincidences,
like some dreams, are
an inseparable part of reality."

Not Another Sting
(for Ben Okri)

26 June 2011

His bag sagging,
Dancing to the tune.

He adjusted his belt, if that could help,
And moves on in that dangerous grip,

Perching on Scorpion's tail,
Searching for rescue.

A spell of biting cold
Deep in his spine,

In noon-day
Surge of tropical heat.

Near-death-experience
Should at that instant

Scorpion turn round
And adds another sting.

Pain

26 June 2011

His puffy head & callous heart
have been a source
of such great pain
for you and me and all.

How dare you stand here now and say
he should be spared
the stinging pain from the leather whip,
to spare us all the rising shame?

Koboko does the trick, you know,
makes him face the shame and stares up
in retrospect, drawing close to face stark reality:
there are greater villains - Death and Pangs of Death.

Pain is such a lesson for you and me;
lifts us up from mire of slumber
makes us dream the future we need to build
and start today to lay the bricks.

It's a greatest lesson for the likes of him;
makes them humble, at least for once,
momentarily wise, and could
some drive permanently sane.

Give him excruciating pain, but kill him not;
let him breathe and feel the tinge of it
and learn, so others like him may follow suit,
so peace may be the brand of air we breathe.

Beware Tyranny

26 June 2011

I foresee Tyranny,
And I warn against political suicide;
It is insanity, not sanity.

I smell Tyranny,
And I sneeze against mental slavery;
It is insanity, not sanity.

I behold Tyranny,
And I morn generational homicide;
It is insanity, not sanity.

I witness Tyranny,
And I bemoan geo-political genocide;
It is insanity, not sanity.

I live Tyranny,
And I decry global villainy;
It is insanity, not sanity.

Multilingualist

26 June 2011

Hypocrite?
What a great name!
With a lot more
Linked to it.

Just Two-pronged Tongue?
Aha, Double-edged Sword!
Double-faced Figure…
So long is the list.

Cite them all?
That could take a year or two!
But, just to add to the list,
I am actually Multilingualist.

Choking Air

26 June 2011

Choking air at home's often hard to withstand,
Ojom's lungs already black like tar,
His chest wheezing with deadly cough,
Sometimes spitting out phlegm of shame,
His tummy often rumbling
At everything he smelt;
It simply was beyond his tolerance limit.

At first cock-crow, he picked his way
Down a heavily littered road
Heading for a city he thought had purer air,
Wading on old plastics, rusting cans, broken bottles;
Kitchen wastes, faeces, carcasses, corpses;
Soldier ants, termites, hermit crabs, scorpions;
Millipedes, centipedes, earth worms, snakes.

But on he went, encountering
The strangest of them all:
An old, wrinkled lady with a long, spiky beard,
An old, stooping man with the face of a bull,
A little boy walking by gliding on his head,
A fair-skinned girl with nostrils towards the sky,
A baby in a tree with snakes for branches.

But on and on he went, down the road,
Encountering much more than ever before:
A very swift river clearly flowing uphill,
A large crocodile with sword for snout,
A little, quirky cat with spears for whiskers,
A stocky elephant with python for trunk,
A multi-fruited tree at the centre of a lake.

But on and on, determined to arrive,
First he met a woman carrying embers on her palms,
Then a group of men sitting round a smoky fire,
Next a maze of caves puffing out jets of fumes,
This right there in the middle of the city;
He stood looking North, South, East and West,
Arms akimbo, wondering what next was best to do.

The Lost Sheep

28 June 2011

It was a long sleep,
Tenaciously deep.

How my head I keep
No drum can beat.

And soon I hear a bleat
Across a carpet of peat.

Strangely I hold a steak,
Unable to eat or speak,

As I face a huge peak
Tall like Sunbird's beak.

Then up the mount so steep,
Climbing as I weep,

Searching for the sheep.
And I get this beep,

Stirring me from the creep.
And I give a long peep

Down the valley deep,
And I see it's the sheep.

Storm

28 June 2011

It started
Like a gentle breeze,
Caressing my cheeks.

Then, in a sudden burst,

It was
A violent, whirly wind
Blowing down mansions of rock,
Tearing up giants of trees.

Just a moment.

Must I have, then, the highway crossed,
Erect like Iroko tree,
Walking, chest out, like Gorilla?

What wiser choice was there?

All around me I saw
Chimps, Buffalos, Elephants, Leopards,
Crocodiles, Giant Pangolins, Giant Lizards,

Even Gorillas, crawling like common lizards.

And on my knees, without delay,
I went,
Creeping like the beasts.

Cry for Help

28 June 2011

His cry for help
Received…
Mocking silence.

His mutilated body laid for public viewing
Received…
Floods of accolades.

His household left behind
Received…
Heavy clenched fists.

But his name left behind remains
A fount that feeds…
Nile, Niger, Congo, Sanaga, Orange, Limpopo, Zambezi.

Waterfall

28 June 2011

Waterfall.
Noisy.
Heard a thousand miles away.
Like colony of weaverbirds
In the heat
Of a great assignment.
Digging even rocks
A thousand times faster
Than a thousand giant rats
Arranged in a fierce competition.
But not as deep as the less noisy ocean.

Waterfall.
Noisy.
Heard a thousand miles away.
Like a thousand caterpillars
On a great mission.
Clearing,
Digging,
Cracking,
Crushing,
Rolling rocks and debris.
But not as retentive as the less noisy ocean.

Saying Goodbye to Hardship

28 June 2011

Just after the desert drill
Each now ready to dodge
Get on board for new land to till
Bearing none at home a grudge

Outside hundreds line up
They know that it is a hard ship
That each will soon drink from silver cup
Saying goodbye to hardship

A Tear So Dear

28 June 2011

Look at the sky
Just like an eye

That can shed a tear
That is so dear

It wears a blue dye
Like eye of a spy

That can shed a tear
That is so dear

One addicted to rye
Ready to wave good-bye

That can shed a tear
That is so dear

The Monster

28 June 2011

We crawl stealthily through your creepy shore
On our way to and from the Mungo for a wash;
You must be such a fearsome beast.

Your voice sends chills down their spine,
Your form can destroy my sight, they say;
You must be such a fearsome beast.

Your hands are a leopard's claws,
Your tongue passes for a scorpion's tail;
You must be such a fearsome beast.

To every seed hatched and nurtured here
A monster qualifies your name;
You must be such a fearsome beast.

I have grown up contemplating your form,
A real monster, from the stories I am told;
You must be such a fearsome beast.

I have never imagined myself alive,
Coming face-to-face with you even in a crowd;
You must be such a fearsome beast.

"Come on, my son, where are you going?"
I turned abruptly and saw a very huge man.
"What's your name, Sir?" "Pa Nkumanang."

Without vacillation, I took to my heels.
"No, my son, don't hurt yourself."
I turned round, facing him, walking backwards.

"That is the name. You are the monster.
I'm not your son, no, I'm not."
"Don't run and hurt yourself, I say."

And I stood and gave him an intent look.
"He doesn't sound like or seem the monster I'm told."
And, bravely, I walked steadily towards him.

He took me in his arms and gave me a big hug.
"You aren't the monster I really want to see."
And the man smiled, "I am the visible monster here."

Thoughts: "Is it the hair?" *Aloud*: "But where's the real one?"
"A hundred more than one monster dwell here,
Which their eyes are not trained enough to spot."

Mother Offy

*(For my daughter Offy, on her success in her
First School Leaving Certificate Examination)*

29 June 2011

O, my mother Offy,
My Korup Queen
Born only yesterday,
Bringing me joy upon joy
Everyday,
From the day you returned to me
To help me build up my home.
O, Offy, you are the best!

O, Mother Offy,
I pray to God to help you
Maintain that spirit of hard work
And academic excellence
So that while in Secondary School
We will have many other opportunities
To celebrate and praise GOD.

Congratulations, my daughter,
Mother Offy, my Korup Queen,
On your success in your
First School Leaving Certificate Examination,
After your pass in List A
In the Common Entrance Examination
And First Position in the Interview at
St. Therese International Comprehensive Secondary School.
GOD BLESS YOU now and forever more. Amen.

Flying like A Bird

30 June 2011

He grew up thinking
He could fly like a bird;
Several times he tried,
Almost crashing on the rocks.

But one bright day
It came out right;
He clicked his feet in a weird, wily way,
Something he can't really recall,

And off the ground he shot into space;
So sure of flight
He went
In that reverie.

In just that maiden flight
He stole the aerial show,
Amongst Eagles, Parrots, and Sparrows,
Flying Squirrels watching timidly from tree trunks.

He flew across a stretch of endless jungle,
Over a sea with a dam to his left,
Then tore through clouds and hovered in the blue,
Alone, amidst some eerie musical sound.

Then on, the skill became a great part of him,
Applying it avidly in climes of threat.
Like, as lad chased by family foes,
And as adult by intimate friends.
Then came that day of dreadful woe,
Armed to the teeth poured in wrathful militia,
Pushed his kin and him up a cliffy mount,
And he clicked his feet…but missed the trick.

Listen To His Statement

30 June 2011

At last he found himself in a most deserved mess,
And decided he shouldn't
The saga cover with a gaudy dress.

"Those three coaxed
Me into drinking a large Guinness.
These three coerced
Me into this under-ground Business."

He was still nude
As he spoke,
Sitting beside a stripped, seven-year-old dude,
His man still nodding as proof it was no joke.

"Listen to yourself, look at you; disgrace, indeed,"
Said a man in black uniforms,
"And since a man your age gives in to such a spiteful deed
You must commence by paying dearly for the forms."

You Are Who You Are

30 June 2011

You are the dazzling Light
Walking the firmament above,
The Light
Over the lands and seas;
The Light
Illuminating the Heavens and the Earth,
The Light
Powering the entire Universe and watching over Earth
And all that on it crawls, walks, swims, and flies.

You are the Light
Here and there at the same time,
In our homes, offices, streets, and gardens;
You are the Light that escapes our human eyes, yet
You are Omnipresent.

You are the Light
We will neither behold nor comprehend, but which
Sees us from out to in, and understands us
To the smallest, finest detail that there is, so
You are Omniscient.

You are the Light
That shows us the right path to take, protecting us,
By pushing all the demons down the abyss,
By crushing all the monsters in our way,
By striking every evil spirit around, therefore
You are Omnipotent.
You are the silent Voice
Whispering into our stubborn ears;
You are the Voice
Floating into our callous hearts,

Instilling us with the spirit of boundless love;
Into our minds, blessing us abundantly
With intellectual prowess and scintillating thought;
Into our dreams, giving us generously
The power of vision and inventive spirit;

You are the Voice
That tells us to help and not to hurt,
The Voice
That brings warring parties to speaking terms.

You are the rescuing Hand
That brings us out of the tunnel of death
And protects us by day and by night,
You are the Hand
That saves us during fire disasters, storms and floods,
The Hand
That sends us sun and rain,
The Hand
That gives us bread day by day,
The Hand
That drives our train, bus and car from A to B,
The Hand
That sails our ship and flies our plane from A to B.

You are the dazzling Light, silent Voice, rescuing Hand;
Omnipresent,
        Omniscient,
                Omnipotent;
                You truly are Who You are.

The Tree

1 July 2011

I
Hear
You sulking
Day and night,
Complaining
About the biting, freezing cold,
About the burning heat, about hunger and
Starvation, you who have legs to run and hands with which
To till and build. Were it that you were me, embracing the
raw Cold
And
Heat
 And
Mad
 Storms
And floods,
Sensing the
Seasons come
 And go, 200
Rounds,
January to
December,
Dancing on the
Same spot under
 The naked sky, giving
Shelter, receiving none,
What story would you tell?

If Only the Right Cream

1 July 2011

O, that we may unearth the precise cream
That constitutes a solid team
Of men that deem
With beam
And dream
And make the engine steam
And us to give that happy scream
As we hear the flow of saving stream
Building conviction our future will gleam

Stench

2 July 2011

Must I crouch,
Donned in sludge-filled suit
Underneath a flamboyant *agbada*,
In scourging,
Tropical heat,
My head,
In gold armour,
To shield,
My lone house to
Shelter,
My progeny
And kin to prop,
Playing
The great spectator
Of nefarious acts of loyalty,
Of treacherous looting,
Of desiccating of the arid
To flood the swampy,
Of thinning of the scanty
To crowd the lushly,
Of humming of anthems
Debouching
Rivers of
Stench to humanity?

Read a Poem

2 July 2011

Read a poem at dusk, and
You achieve intellectual growth;
This is self-enriching medium.

Read a poem at dawn, and
You ensure your mental health;
This is self-sanitising frame.

Read a poem at noontime, and
You guarantee your moral sanity;
This is self-expurgating bleach,
An aid for you to play well your great societal role.

Read a poem, for poetry is
A fount of tonic, flowing in
Meandering twists and turns,
Or in frothing cascades wild,

At the surface of a pool it rests,
Like clear cream on tepid water,
In the ocean floor it sleeps
Like dense ice cubes, freezing cold;

It may be sweet or bitter; bland, harsh or acidic,
But ponder again;
It may be the last scion
To save
Society's vanishing cream.

His Choice

2 July 2011

With him she picked endless quarrels
Even when he brought news of laurels;
Often she started a hateful fight
Even in the dead of night,
But, still, she remained his choice.

Clearly she'd been groomed also to live on lies,
A thousand threats from clients they'd cast the dice;
This had brought her man untold troubles,
As oft he had to pay her fines in doubles,
But, still, she remained his choice.

A story is told of her double dealings;
Her business was known for triple billings,
Most clients had turned their backs on her shop,
Yet she would find no reason the tricks to stop,
But, still, she remained his choice.

Her timeless tricks had ruined her business,
A ruin that brought her untold financial stress;
Her incessant disposition earned her a sue for divorce,
And now she'd engaged a solicitor in discourse,
In hopes she'd regain her place as his choice.

The Guided Tour

2 July 2011

Altogether we were a family of four,
First time in Africa, on a guided tour.

The first stop was to see some popular caves,
But he drove us to a sea of renowned graves.

Next we had to buy a painting of a desert,
But he took us where to buy some coloured dessert.

There was a plan to visit a certain Indian,
But he gave us a horrible ride to Ndian.

We decided we should climb the Rumpi Hill,
But he drove us where we had to go down and till.

We decided we should take the children for some cones,
But he treated us to a spicy meal of strange, hard bones.

Finally, he had to take us where to rest,
But, first, he treated us to a hilarious jest.

Maybe my accent was strangely strong,
Or my semantics confusingly wrong.

Maybe we hired a professional clown,
Who decided to wear our tour a floral crown.

Fierce Theatre Animal

2 July 2011

A
Fierce
Theatre animal
He turns out to be,
Or so he's branded
Mostly by those at power helm;

His diction is anger-laden,
Yes;
His décor too morbid,
True;
His message rather pointed,
No objection;
His tone largely unforgiving,
Perhaps;

But
Still, I
Think he wins,
As he's fiercely kind,
Morally decent,
Incarnating Justice,
Pricking consciences,
Rocking the land,
Inspiring the masses
To useful wealth creation,
Directing political change,
Prompting wealth redistribution,
Guaranteeing sustainable economic development.

Bent to Bite

4 July 2011

It immediately became clear to me
It wasn't a spray of love
But a dash for gold
She thought
Was buried in my bag of fame
And I cut the pulpy cord abruptly
Lest time turned it into a steel rod
And she was bent on biting my nose

She went for the lips
And not for the heart
I learnt she had jumped from
Flower to flower
In that queer game
And was casted a hundredfold
So I had to cut the cord before it was night
And she was bent on biting my nose

She despoiled my water source
Ravaged my garden
Broke my pots and plates
Yet unsatisfied
She was bent on biting my nose

Many seasons had come and gone
And she had found a tall tree on which to lean
And I had lost memory of her
And I thought she had of me
But yet
She was bent on biting my nose
Under the tree I sat
Like others

Tilling
To escape the heat of time
And the tree gave off a branch just above my head
And I jumped aside
Watching the weak weapon in disdain
And the tree created a huge gap
Letting in a stream of harsh sun rays where I sat
As she was still bent on biting my nose

I gave a hard blow with a tiny pen
Not to her
But the tree on which she leaned
And it was a mighty fall
Accompanied by endless yelling
As there were gory injuries sustained
Even by that whore
I knew she leaning on that tree
Was strongly behind the nefarious act
As she was still bent on biting my nose

Get a New Machete

4 July 2011

To old wounds give proper dressings;
Wait to receive abundant blessings.

Never acid should be your heart's portion;
Nor your hands concoct strange potion.

Come on, bury that old, strange hatchet;
Rush to market and get new machete.

Move away from that dead yesterday;
Yield not to any undue delay.

Give the wounds some real clean dressings;
Wait and you'll get all the blessings.

Ingredients of Youth

4 July 2011

Passionate love
Burning wild and blind;
Anger
Blowing tempest toss;
Vanity
Like modelled belle,
Parading nude,
Displaying elegance;
Jealousy
Clear acid bitter and sour;
Rowdiness
Qua Falls is no compare;
Horn-locking,
Like he-goat peeing,
Minute by minute.

Love in Haste

4 July 2011

Up from opposite end
He strolled to her on the dancing floor.
It started with exchange of "hi", and
Built into a dance
And a warm hug,
So quick,
Like people who had met before.
Then passionate staring into the eyes,
And suddenly into a long, wet kiss.
And then another dance
Taking them into a bed next door.
And next into a ready bed
Where, for years, she lay,
Now looking like a *suicide model*,
Unwilling to go on routine parades.
John quite healthy and away,
Perhaps, another rounds he went,
While her dad was pinned down
To pawn his only farm
To pay the price.

African Time

4 July 2011

African beauty
Stays, unchanging,
Steady and sure,
Evading
Blemishes from season's toll.
But
African time
So erratic, so elastic,
Evolving
Minute by minute,
Losing taste and lustre.

Waiting for the Occasion

4 July 2011

20th May or so, and everyone was there,
Waiting for the occasion to start,
Time set at 10 a.m.

But that was only
Good time for him to take his bath
Before his hot breakfast steady and sure.

The MC was almost on his second
Round of the martial tunes,
It was now 1 p.m.

His driver who sat
At the steering
Now produced a heavy nasal tune on it.

"Get up, you fool," shouted he, and driver shook in fear.
It was now 2 p.m., and to get him to his seat,
It took us another ten minutes.

The ride was slow and steady,
With escorts at the fore and at the rear,
And traffic cleared the way for him.

Escorts on siren-blasting like thunderbolts on a stormy day,
Taking him there at 3 p.m. to meet, for the first time,
Gaping chairs and dancing grasshoppers monopolising the field.

Pocket Wash

4 July 2011

10 a.m., and he had already got his pay,
Now safe in his coat pocket.

Before his thought for home to dash
He had to go for routine throat wash.

There he got, once again, into body massage,
Which mellowed into TTT (tongue-to-tongue) exercise.

His suit he took off at once for full massage,
Savouring it into a long, deep sleep.

10 p.m. took him home, and he saw in his clear eyes
He also had a clear first-class pocket wash.

Pa Hardship Is Dead-o!

5 July 2011

Pa Hardship is dead-o!

O, what a generous donor you were!
You left no household untouched.

Pa Hardship is dead-o!

Your hand of magnanimity always stretched,
Even to those who worked hard not to receive.

Pa Hardship is dead-o!

Who must have murdered you, Pa Hardship,
You, the bitter leaf seller?

Pa Hardship is dead-o!

Our bitter leaf kiosk is gone,
Replaced by groceries of salads, sandwiches, and hamburgers.

Pa Hardship is dead-o!

Who must have murdered you, Pa Hardship,
You, the palm oil trader?

Pa Hardship is dead-o!

Our palm oil market is gone,
Replaced by supermarkets of vegetable oils of assorted types.

Pa Hardship is dead-o!

Who must have murdered you, Pa Hardship,
You, the palm wine merchant?

Pa Hardship is dead-o!

Our palm wine shed is gone,
Replaced by beer parlours and wine and whisky shops.

Pa Hardship is dead-o!

O, Pa Hardship The Generous, we miss you-o!
But, please, as you go, don't turn your face behind!

Pa Hardship is dead-o!

Stage Paradox

6 July 2011

You announce to the whole wide world,
In trumpet blast;
You wear a human heart;
You sing to them,
In divine melody,
Endless songs of love;
But I see in that chest of yours
The devil's club.

You proclaim yourself,
In earnest sincerity,
A lover of peace:
You preach the gospel of unity
Amongst men;
You declare you're out
To pull polar races together,
But clearly I see you
Carrying
The devil's dividing sword.

You display,
In open market
And worship places and festivals,
The generosity of your hands;
You shower on them flakes of alms,
In ceaseless avalanche,
But you give to them less than half
What you stole from them the other day.

Dangerous Reactions

6 July 2011

He uses a catapult and hurls pebbles
Against a hard rock
Opposite his resting stool
To display his shooting skill;

And splashes oil-stained water
Against a wall next to the stool on which he rests
Wearing an agbada
Made of fine, white cotton material;

He spits into the air
Above his head
Wearing a white, title cap
After a generous meal of cola nuts;

Sometimes he strives to kill
Persistent mosquitoes hovering around his children
With a heavy machine gun
On the slightest provocation;

One day he tried
To use a machete to cut into two halves
A nasty worm wriggling on his bare left thigh
As expression of his total disgust for the disrespectful act;

The other day
He smashed his plate of food
With a heavy wooden club
In a bid to kill a fly that rudely perched on his food
Two nights before
He shattered his old-fashioned, legendary parlour lamp
With his staff

When a cockroach lingered about it in an upsetting flight

This time he has used very toxic chemicals
To destroy some stubborn, invasive grass
Near his community's only source of drinking water
To prevent the lush at the first showers of rain

Looking For a Job

7 July 2011

Looking for a job
I was asked twice
To pay a fee
Way higher than
My total school expenditure.

Looking for a job
I was asked twice
To come back later, later,
As my name sounds different from theirs.

Looking for a job
I was raped twice
On bare office tables,
As remedy for my pass degree.

Cruel Invitation

11 July 2011

I watched his uneasy strides,
So unsteady as he walked in
Bringing me such prime honour to your fort,
And my picky funnels
Amplified the massive storm
Breathing in the solemn depth
Of his ocean floor.

I saw your lips issuing, as I walked in,
Bubbles of gold in the dying glow
As you chattered welcomingly, embracing me,
But I could feel the tsunami
Swelling dangerously
In the cavity
Of that rock beneath.

I heard your breath puffing in ceaseless floods,
Venting soothing notes of magnanimity
Condensing and growing into glittering balls of delight
Beneath the stupendous glory of the setting sun,
But I could behold the jagged chisels beneath
Oozing, in stealthy spurts,
The lethal venom of a serpent's fangs.

I watched him setting, in utmost alacrity,
Such enticing dinner prepared at your behest,
But I could sense, with intuitive certainty,
The toxin running in tumultuous ripples,
The veins of those cans cackling in cruel candour;
And I contrived my unrestrained exit,
Early enough to flee in a sudden gush of psychopathic fit.

Crumbs for Gold

14 July 2011

He knows you've lived
A thousand seasons in the show,
Sustained a myriad insults in the race,
Like the coaching you've received;

He knows you've snatched
A gold trophy or more
And that you are
By no means
Less than heavyweight,
Nor have a match as mentor in the show.

He knows you keep a string of mouths
Yawning daily for mouthfuls,
Knowing your shine of gold
Will bring them more tons by-and-by;

He knows you'd been a jaguar
In the fending race,
Though now your feet feel
So leaded from the strain of time.

All this he remembers daily
As he beholds your shrivelled face
Sitting on that lowly stool,
On that wobbling, naked place
That barely supports your weight and might,
Waiting for the flaky crumbs
As the moon shuts her eyes in the doze.
All this he's contrived
With dexterity
And delightful pride;

And given you
That humble stool and crumbs
Adding more slices to his from left to right
So his height remains conspicuously royal,
Enough to smother yours and makes you appear dwarf
And shades your gold from every giant's sight.

But he's been watched all along
In this ugly, mean game of his,
And now he knows and fears
The shame and pain he's kept for you
Will soon be spent
And that your gold will shine even more
And attract you more gold by-and-by
While his the shame and pain he dished for you.

Too Hard To Crack

21 July 2011

      I see an old tree swaying solo on the stormy cliff,
         With fibrous roots
Set entirely on rocks too hard to crack,
         Humus integration into the systems sporadically
blocked,
      Ensuring no constant growth, not even of itself,
         Famished saplings fleeing to copious soils.

Talking Into Space

21 July 2011

Sound of music,
And a small device ensued from his pocket,
His old mum already dancing to the tune.
"Hello, brother," and his Mum ceased the dance,
Stood gawking at him, wondering in trepidation
Why the queer posture - his fist planted against his ear.
"Right at home, brother. Mean right in the village!
Surprise, indeed, brother. How is London?"
"Which brother, son, talking into space?
And what the hell with London?"
"No interloping, Mum,
It's quite a fortune for the call."

Silence.

"Talking to inquisitive Mum, brother.
How did it happen? Waves' generosity, brother.
Contemporary services
Carried to the far reaches of the globe!"

Silence.

"Exactly! A small but smart and potent device
Saying no to tribalism,
Saying no to nepotism, saying no to favouritism,
Saying no to many more such isms as those above,
And a big no to the serpentine, egocentric
River that chooses where to flow."
Silence.

"She's in top form, brother, quite strong,
And standing right next to me as I speak.

Beg your pardon?
How can that be done?
My knowledge of modernity cries for help, poor me."

Silence.

"Western what? OK, got it.
Will be right there next week.
And what digits in the deal?

Silence.

Got it. OK, details by text.

Silence.

"Gratitude, brother, a lot of it;
That'll be a huge weight off the spider,
The legend renowned for carrying loads solo."
His fist left his ear,
And he heaved a sigh of relief,
And his mum asked to know:
"Are you alright, son,
After such an awkward, pendulum-dance
To silent music, I suppose,
Talking into space?"

Too Strong a Character

24 July 2011

He's so
Renowned,
Powerful, clever, gifted, affluent, fluent,
Diligent and travelled, which makes me empty,
Baseless, weightless, wingless, helpless.

He is
Resistance,
Often too proud, which makes me
So uneasy under his breath,
Shivering freely when in ring with him;
He's too strong a character for me.

He's
So smart,
Too strong a character, which makes me
Tremble when he's in a public show
And mine is a prime role to play;
He's too strong a character for me.

So I grew
Weedy and wily,
Crude and cruel,
And concocted a gift,
A potion too potent for him:
Gossiping, backbiting and backstabbing,
Spawning curses, hardship, doom and gloom,
Poisonous arrows, missiles, and an exquisite coffin
Dressed in a golden shell of dozens of cold crocodile tears.

Press to Express

6 August 2011

I guess by now you've found an armour-dress
Ready and set for the 8:8 Congress
There to bandy words over a Guinness
A novel way to start a big business

Solidarity struggle to redress
Everyone swearing never to transgress
But old transgressions ready to confess
New contrivances ever to suppress

Forget you not your greatest role to press
Our collective views written to express
A few salient points marshalled to buttress
Revealing both our fusion and distress

Prove you rise above a novice actress
Enraged but meticulously fearless
Sure yet again the huge crowd to impress
And place a golden crown on our fortress

Three Tiny Ticks

27 August 2007

Two dog-nostrils one quarter smell,
Four human-pairs two quarters do;
Two owl-ears one quarter hear,
Four lizard-pairs two quarters do;
Two eagle-eyes one quarter see,
Four bat-pairs two quarters do –
These popular anecdotes soon became

As once upon a time, the story goes,
Thrice three tiny chicks,
Branded Three Tiny Ticks,
Smelled the presences of three deadly hawks
And each time lead their sibling-chicks, they themselves
Not left to danger under the open sky,
Into Mother-hen's shelter-wings they all rushed,
Surely the shield to wear.

But this as signal should also have served
For Mother-hen with such display of wits,
But now gripped by such arrogance
The warning signs completely she ignored,
Dismissed these by simple fact from 3-Ts they emanated,
Individuals who though thrice she allowed to enjoy
Together with their big-but-witless sibling-chicks
The assured safety under her fortified shield.

So shielded was Mother-hen herself by her weight,
Apparent from her height and enormous bulk,
That Deadly Hawks feared their wings and claws they could
Lose should each such great bulk strive to lift;
And knowledge of this Mother-hen had firm grip
Thus her arrogance surely tripled thrice,
Blinding her to obvious menacing schemes.

Next was visitation by a tiny, witty hawk,
Too minute in form Mother-hen he dares not face,
But so dauntless in mind the hypothesis he's poised to test,
To bring to light the assumed correlation,
The much-celebrated link between bulk, height and weight,
And 3-Ts so played their part
The deadly intrigue clearly to announce,
But Mother-hen still on fearless ground stood firm.

And in a twinkle Tiny Hawk a swift descent made,
And see how Mother-hen was lifted with ease,
By the use of wit, not of might,
Her bulk now seeming merely of feathers made,
Especially as 3-Ts she dropped on stubbornness' grounds
Dozen Greats now chuckling with joyful security
Under her mammoth protective wings,
Tickled, as it were, by airborne glides and jerks,
Flight they were certain was to surer safety headed
As pilot, to them, was none but Mother-hen.

Don't Let Her Sink

11 September 2011

When daily complaints fill
Your cherished cup of drink;
And each day your name wears
Such a thick coat of soot;

When curses hit your bank
Like heinous waves the shore,
Day by day true friends fleeing
As dreadful foes flood in;

When storms rage and threaten,
Some roofs flying in pieces,
The anguish to assuage,
Bow, yield to their behest;

When life's melody fades
Into melancholy
And all your dreams seem lost,
Your ship in eddy caught;

Step out and take a look
Where in your ship there're holes,
Before a rush of flood
That can cause her to sink.

Beyond Human Destruction

13 September 2011

Sometimes I sit solo in the dark and ponder and wonder
How much more lies buried within the core of Cosmos
Un-smelled by human instincts
Unpicked by human senses and lenses
Undreamt by human brain and vision
Inconceivable by human imagination
Un-foretold by prophets past and present
So far beyond human ingenuity
Far beyond that wild well of imagination
Though now crystallized in great abilities
(As measured by human standards)
Displayed in Science and Technology
Summarised in great civilisations
Showcasing mounts of great inventions
(As rated by human measurements)
Yet below that realm of activity and energy
With power to ignite and prompt an Eco-quake
To incite intergenerational communication
That culminates in a lasting convention of peace
With cosmic, astrological and planetary forces
That celebrate both celestial and terrestrial life
See the forces hovering in the seamless blue above
And buried deep in the core of the massive ball of gold
The fiery ball that sits fixed on that primordial stool
Yet bouncing daily from East to West
In turbulent and voluptuous gyrations
Stretching or flinging its arms in ceaseless splash of life
Picking up and consuming in utter voraciousness
Every sprawling creature within its radius of lethality
From the macroscopic to the microscopic, barring the cosmic
Yet providing the fount of the soothing fire of green
Emitting dust not only of life but of immortality

Celestial particles that at this juncture
(If the human ear were trained for silent voices to hear)
Should have permeated the entire Universe
Filled the air sacs of Atmosphere
Flushed the cholesterol-blocked vessels of Troposphere
Inundated the fatal germs in the gaping canals of Jealousy
Reclaimed the yawning cesspools of greed
Demolished the tortuous dams of selfishness
And decimated all vestiges of Ego-systems
While fussily tending the even plains of Ecosystems
Thus giving our ailing Mother Earth
And every creature that on it now prowls in uncertainty
The immutable covering of cosmic dust
Particles lased with enamel of boundless, celestial love
Wrapped in the swaddling cloth of humility
Devoid of nepotism, tribalism, elitism, racism
Love which defines our common sense of purpose and fulfilment
And provides resistance even to rapid mutational processes
And to impacts of free ultraviolet rays from Cosmos
And to impacts of fatal particles from atomic bombs
And to impacts of some unknown Weapons of Mass Destruction
Fuel that sparks constructive visions that drive positive actions
That covers Mother Earth and all about her in amour of steel
A new flesh-and-blood coating of particles beyond transmutation
Beyond destruction by human intrigues and inventions